Published by Independent Television Publications Ltd.,
for Independent Television Books Ltd.,
247 Tottenham Court Road, London W1P 0AU, England.

Printed and bound in Great Britain by
Morrison & Gibb Ltd., London and Edinburgh

ISBN 0 900727 74 8

Look-in TELEVISION ANNUAL

Contents

Cover illustration by Arnaldo Putzu

During the recent sci-fi boom we've seen lots of impressive hardware on our screens, from Han Solo's *Millenium Falcon* (Star Wars) to the Battlestar Galactica itself, from the *USS Cygnus* (The Black Hole) to the pulsating sounds and flashing lights of the alien craft in Close Encounters Of The Third Kind. We've even had 'people' made out of bits of ironmongery—R2-D2 and C-3PO (from Star Wars, of course), Muffitt (Battlestar Galactica) Vincent (The Black Hole) and lots more. But sci-fi has also brought us flesh and blood (well, almost!) super-heroes too. So let's forget the machinery and concentrate on those characters who are truly . . .

LARGER THAN LIFE!

Superman—Christopher Reeve

Lou Ferrigno as *The Incredible Hulk*.

WHAM! POW! THUD! With all the power of a bulldozer, Superman hits out against his evil foe. A final, mighty blow—ZADONK!—and another baddie bites the dust—the world can sleep easy tonight! How dull life would be without the super-heroes like Superman. Secretly, we love to imagine ourselves as the super-hero; strong as an ox; incredibly handsome and winning the admiration of everyone by ridding the world of evil characters almost every time we turn a corner.

For the fictional super-heroes we see on TV and in the cinema, you really have to thank comics in general and a man named Jerry Siegel in particular. He was the guy who wrote Superman, the original comic-book hero, who has since appeared in radio serials, animated cartoons and, of course, **Superman—The Movie** and the forthcoming **Superman II**.

Superman originated on the planet Krypton—a world doomed to explode, so Superman's (real name Kal-El) father builds a space-ship to jet him to a safer place, namely Earth. To disguise his alien identity on Earth, Kal-El becomes an ordinary, rather dull reporter called Clark Kent, but he uses his super-human strength and powers for the benefit of mankind, as the Superman we all know and love! No doubt it is this double identity that endeared him to the public—in real life his fans were simply Clark Kents—but in their dreams they could halt racing expresses with one hand, and leap across rivers and skyscrapers.

So Superman, born by the pen of Jerry Siegel and artist Joe Schuster in 1933, spawned a whole new breed of comic-book do-gooders. There was Captain America, a mere human who was given a new lease of super-life with an injected strength-serum. In 1939 came Batman (really millionaire Bruce Wayne) and his sidekick Robin, who fought such festering fiends as the Joker, the Penguin and that foul feline, Cat Woman. Bruce Wayne turned from being a playboy to a crimefighter, so the story goes, after his parents were murdered on the way home from a movie. (Whether or not it was a **Superman** movie the story doesn't say!)

But Batman differs from Superman in that he uses no supernatural powers. Instead, he uses his supreme knowledge to outwit criminals, assisted by a variety of technological wonders such as the Batcomputer, Batmobile and Batcopter—all built without the aid of silicon chips! But there seems to be no valid explanation for the caped-crusader's strange costume, especially when Robin comes out with lines like: *"We must try to look inconspicuous"* —in the middle of Gotham City's main street!

In the 1960s **Batman** ⟫⟫ ➤

Lynda Carter as *Wonder Woman*.

Bill Bixby and Lou Ferrigno—*The Hulk* before and after.

Adam West as *Batman*.

came to TV, portrayed by Adam West, complete with very convincing reconstructions of the Batcave (Bruce Wayne's cellar play-room) and the Batmobile.

Another comic-book hero to make a successful transgression to TV was the female version of Superman—**Wonder Woman,** played by Lynda Carter. The original Wonder Woman comic strip made its debut as long ago as 1942, the idea of a psychologist named William Moulton Marston. Despite being quite a good-looker, Wonder Woman isn't treated at all charmingly by her male foes; and she always gives as good as she gets, in her characteristic unladylike way!

The three main characters you've met so far originated in the stable of DC Comics, Inc., but another major comics group which can be congratulated for producing a wealth of heroic crime-fighters is Marvel Comics and chief writer Stan Lee. Most famous of all the Marvel mighty-men is the Hulk who, when in his 'passive' state is well-mannered Bruce Banner, but is unable to stop himself turning into the muscle-bound Hulk, whose table-manners leave a lot to be desired. How many shirts the poor guy gets through is anybody's guess!

The comic version of the Hulk suggests that the reason for Bruce Banner's uncontrollable 'change-over' is the result of being bombarded by rays from a gamma bomb, but in the popular TV series (and the Universal picture) he subjects himself to gamma radiation in search of an answer as to why strength can come to people under stress, but didn't come to him when he needed to rescue his wife from a burning car.

Incidentally, in the TV series Bruce Banner is renamed Dr. David Banner (played by Bill Bixby, who turns into fellow actor Lou Ferrigno as the strongman Hulk). 28-year-old Lou is a lofty 6ft. 5in. tall, by the way, but green isn't his favourite colour!

Another Marvel super-hero—Spider-Man—has found renewed fame on the large screen, in the film **Spider-Man** and its sequel **Spider-Man Strikes Back,** with Nicholas Hammond in the lead role. Like Clark Kent, Spider-Man when out-of-uniform is a seven-stone weakling, named Peter Parker. But pimply-Pete is bitten by a radioactive spider and suddenly gains the powers of the creature. He can spin a web of immense strength and climb walls but, deep down, still has the problems of an insecure teenager.

Most comic super-heroes are American—with one notable exception. British kids who paid out the exorbitant sum of three (old) pence in 1950 for the new comic **Eagle** were treated to the weekly adventures of Dan Dare—the "pilot of the future". For Dan it wasn't necessary to change into a funny costume in order to right wrongs; he simply jetted around the universe tackling baddies in a space rocket that, these days, looks rather old fashioned for a "pilot of the future".

You might have been surprised, reading this article, to find out just how old all the comic super-heroes are. Even if you think that Buck Rogers and one of the screen's latest super-men, **Flash Gordon,** are new creations, then you're wrong! They were both being followed avidly by kids in the 1930s.

Flash Gordon, written by Alex Raymond, is the story of the continuing fight against Ming the Merciless, who from the planet Mongo, is intent on conquering Earth. Flash is assisted by his girlfriend Dale Arden and scientist Dr. Zarkov in his battles with shark-men, fire-dragons and a variety of alien monsters—all controlled by dastardly Ming.

Flash is now a veteran of the silver screen; **Flash Gordon,** a Universal cinema series, was released in 1936, followed by **Flash Gordon's**

Dr. Zarkov (Frank Shannon), Dale Arden (Jean Rogers) and Buster Crabbe as Flash Gordon in *Flash Gordon's Trip To Mars.*

Trip to Mars in 1938 and, two years later, **Flash Gordon Conquers the Universe.** And 1980, of course, saw the production of a new, improved film by Dino De Laurentiis.

In the most recent **Flash Gordon** epic, Flash himself is played by Sam Jones and his girlfriend by Melody Anderson, while Ming the Merciless is played by Max Von Sydow.

Another comparatively recent revival is Buck Rogers, who made his first comic-strip appearance in early 1929. Buck is a former World War I fighter pilot who is trapped in a mine cave-in. A strange case of sleep-walking through time means that Buck wakes up in the 25th century, where he quickly adapts his bi-plane piloting skills to those of captaining a space cruiser! This Phil Nowlan strip was turned into a movie serial in 12 episodes by Universal in 1939, but not revived on the screen until a new production was spawned by an American TV company in 1978.

We don't want you to believe that there are no new super-heroes. Nor have all of them progressed from comics to films or TV—in fact for some the reverse is the case. One that springs to mind is Gerry Anderson's TV puppet creation of the late sixties, **Captain Scarlet,** who found his way from TV into the comic **TV21.** Scarlet was haunted by the words of the Mysterons: *"This is the voice of the Mysterons. We know you can hear us!"* The Mysterons were aliens who planted human look-alikes on Earth in order to destroy the world. Seemingly, it was only Captain Scarlet

who could search out these aliens and, ultimately, destroy them.

Then, of course, there was that heart-throb star of TV **The Six Million Dollar Man,** alias Steve Austin, who with **The Bionic Woman** (Jaime Sommers) even made the comic-strip pages of **Look-in.** Steve Austin, as portrayed by Lee Majors, represents the super-hero of the late seventies. Gone are the outlandish costumes of Superman and Batman; gone are the corny lines like *"Holy gobstoppers!"* and gone are the duels with mad scientists who want to rule the world. Instead, we saw a human just like you or I; a man〉〉〉〉→

Nicholas Hammond —Spider-Man— strikes out.

Gil Gerard as *Buck Rogers.*

⫸⟩ whose super powers were gained by a combination of medical science and electronic technology. The blue-print for the Supermen of the future? Indeed, with present-day scientists announcing that soon they will be able to plant mini-computers into people's heads to improve their brain-power, it may not be long before we can all be like Batman or Wonder Woman!

Steve Austin was the man we would all like to be. He could exceed the speed limit on foot; he could see long-distance better than an eagle; and could jump higher than a kangaroo. But all these powers cost money—bionic eyes, legs, arms and so on don't come cheap. The price tag is six million dollars, including surgeon's fees of course! Said Majors: *"We use the bionic limbs as much as possible, but still keep the human element, so I don't get compared to Batman. I think you can believe the guy—he has feelings"*.

But even when you're a super-hero, things can go wrong. During the filming of **Six Million Dollar Man,** there were some infuriating moments for Lee. A giant iron bar that he was supposed to snap in half would refuse to bend; or a wall that he was supposed to demolish would stubbornly stand firm. In cases such as those, the film crew would burst into laughter.

Lee's duff takes illustrate that even super-heroes have their "Achilles' heel". As Edward Montagne, producer of **Spider-Man Strikes Back** commented: *"Spider-Man isn't perfect. As a matter of fact, he's not always sure what to do with his super powers—he makes mistakes."*

A super-hero of sorts who makes more mistakes than most is the bumbling Captain Kremmen, alias radio and TV joker Kenny Everett. Kenny makes no secret of the fact that Kremmen is the hero of his childhood fantasies . . . regularly getting beaten-up at school does make you wish you could annihilate your foe by simply sticking your finger up your nose. Kremmen is a send-up of all the super-heroes rolled into one. It's also the formula that took Mork to such fame in the TV series **Mork & Mindy.** Both prove that the job of taking on alien cultures need not be treated all that seriously.

Six Million Dollar Man Steve Austin (Lee Majors).

(Left) Mysteron fighter *Captain Scarlet.* (Right) Comic super-hero *Captain Kremmen.*

Ready for action—*Buck Rogers* (Gil Gerard).

The caped crusader of
Gotham City—*Batman* (Adam West).

My wife's so ugly
that peeping toms
knock on our door
and ask us to
close the curtains.

★★★★★★★★

Q) What do you give a duck
for breakfast?
A) Quacker oats.

Q) What's green,
hairy and wears
sunglasses?
A) A gooseberry
on holiday.

LAUGH-IN

First Tonsil:
What are you getting
all dressed up for?
Second Tonsil:
Oh, the doctor is
taking me out tonight.

★★★★★★★★

Waiter, waiter, will
my omelette be long?
No, sir, round.

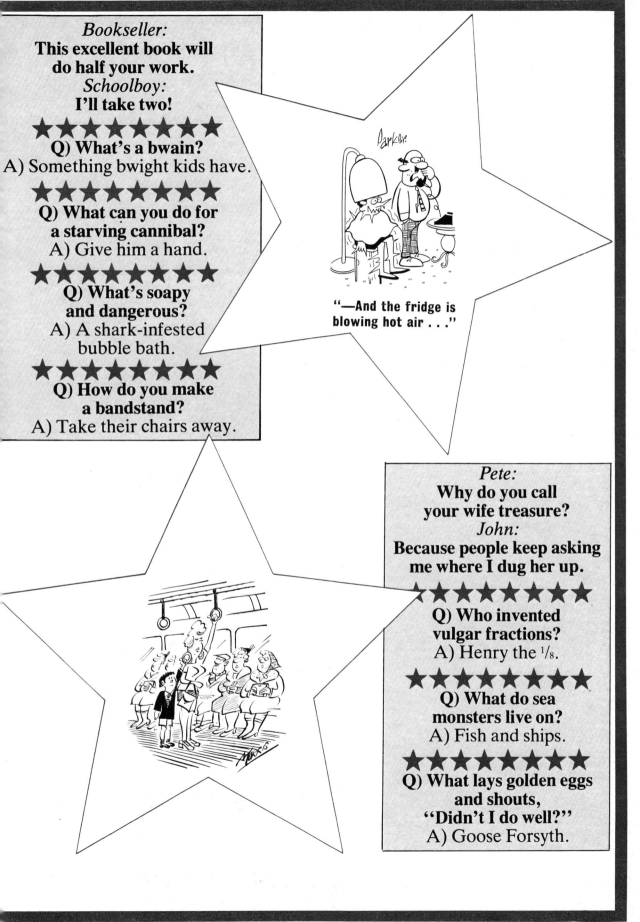

Bookseller:
This excellent book will do half your work.
Schoolboy:
I'll take two!

★★★★★★★★★★

Q) What's a bwain?
A) Something bwight kids have.

★★★★★★★★★★

Q) What can you do for a starving cannibal?
A) Give him a hand.

★★★★★★★★★★

Q) What's soapy and dangerous?
A) A shark-infested bubble bath.

★★★★★★★★★★

Q) How do you make a bandstand?
A) Take their chairs away.

"—And the fridge is blowing hot air . . ."

Pete:
Why do you call your wife treasure?
John:
Because people keep asking me where I dug her up.

★★★★★★★★★★

Q) Who invented vulgar fractions?
A) Henry the $\frac{1}{8}$.

★★★★★★★★★★

Q) What do sea monsters live on?
A) Fish and ships.

★★★★★★★★★★

Q) What lays golden eggs and shouts, "Didn't I do well?"
A) Goose Forsyth.

KENNY EVERETT

Before Kenny Everett made his name as a radio DJ, he was just plain Maurice Cole.

Says Kenny, *"When I went to a pirate radio station, we all had to change our names for legal reasons. I chose Everett after one of my favourite movie actors, Edward Everett Horton. He was a star from the twenties to the forties, an American comic who made loads of films. Kenny just sounded jolly and friendly to go with it."*

Kenny became a DJ at the age of twenty, and although he quickly made a name for himself, his madcap antics often had him falling foul of his employers resulting in the sack on more than one occasion. It wasn't until Kenny joined the team at London's Capital Radio that he began to settle down (for the time being at least!) and finally made a success for himself on TV.

Explains Kenny, *"Over ten years I did lots of shows for TV, but somehow they were never quite right. On my first TV shows, I would forget about the cameras. I would dream up stunts. Then I would wander off, acting the fool, and expect the cameras to follow me around."*

But with Thames Television's **The Kenny Everett Video Show** everything fell perfectly into place. Continues Kenny, *"I'm still surprised that we've managed to get so many big name pop stars on the show—and they let me do the most outrageous things to them. For instance, we had Cliff Richard on one show and we hung him up by his thumbs. A cliff-hanger, get it?*

"I think the stars come on my show because they know they won't get the same old routine nonsense."

They've always been the most easily identifiable members of their respective groups. They've been the ones jostling for position in the world of pop as one decade ended and another starts. Unlike, say, The Beatles (who, in their time, were very much a foursome without one 'star') they're the personalities who tend to be photographed and written about and quoted more than their colleagues. In their own different ways, they're each the . . .

LEADER OF THE GANG

(Left) Debbie Harry.
(Below) Chrissie Hynde.

Some of the current leaders of the gangs are the focus of attention for obvious reasons—they are the recently emerged girl rock stars who have added an extra spark of glamour and style to their bands.

The most written about, photographed and revered on posters stuck to a million bedroom walls is Debbie Harry of Blondie. Being blonde and beautiful makes Debbie an automatic centre of attraction in the group, even though they all desperately claim that they ARE a band, and not just backing musicians for her.

In spite of all the claims, she is always in the spotlight because she is also the band's vocalist and automatically commands attention.

Britain's own blonde bombshell,

Annie Lennox, has become peroxide top of the pops with Th Tourists, but she, too, maintain that she is merely one member of group who have their own collectiv identity. As she only shares lea vocals and also plays keyboards an flute, her claim is probably mor justified.

While another girl who has com forward as the image of her band i Chrissie Hynde of The Pretenders Chrissie used to be a writer on on of the top rock music papers, so sh certainly knew a lot about the musi business—and about publicity— before she launched into her ne career.

She has not given up writing though, for she now writes much c her band's material and was cc

(Left) Annie Lennox.
(Below) Ian Page fronting Secret Affair.

(Right) Freddie Mercury.

...Composer of The Pretenders' first British number one, **Brass in Pocket.**

Which brings us to another group of band leaders who stand out in their own particular crowd. Song writers in bands instantly attract interest, and if the writer is also lead singer there is twice as much chance that they will be singled out for recognition.

Bob Geldof of the Boomtown Rats was responsible for writing hits like **I Don't Like Mondays** and **Rat Trap,** and his flamboyant life style with his girlfriend Paula Yates has consistently pushed him into the limelight, like Mick Jagger of The Rolling Stones before him—whose footsteps Bob seems to be following closely.

Two more singer/songwriters whose names have been as well known as those of their groups are Queen's Freddie Mercury, and Gary Numan who dropped the Tubeway Army band name, to become better known as a solo artist.

They've both been the focal point of stage shows, although their styles contrast vividly. Freddie poses and preens his way through Queen's set, while Gary tries to retain a moody, dark and distant image. Yet both approaches seem to have the same effect on ecstatic followers.

It's no secret that Secret Affair's inspiration has been Ian Page, who's claimed to have almost single-handedly brought about a mod music revival. Ian's not only

had a hand in writing his group's material, he also brought the band together and formed his own record company to release their work. He is an artist who richly deserved to emerge from the shadows of group identity. So did Richard Jobson, driving force of The Skids, co-writer of their material and thus partly responsible for **Into The Valley, Masquerade** and others.

There's also Jimmy Pursey, the Hersham Boy himself, whose antics have made him a rebellious symbol at the front of Sham 69, and to a certain extent Joe Strummer has had the same amount of influence over his band, The Clash—but when it comes to their respective groups' music, both Jimmy and Joe collaborate with other band members.

We must not forget John Lydon, either, whose individuality has made him the power behind two bands, Public Image Limited, and (as Johnny Rotten) The Sex Pistols.

Public Image proved vital to another group leader who's not only sung and written his band's material, but also played an instrument—Sting of The Police, who could justifiably be called the male equivalent of Debbie Harry. The other members of The Police, Stewart Copeland and Andy Sum-

mers, agree that bass player Sting has been primarily responsible for the group's astonishing rise to fame and he's said that he could not have played his part without them.

Paul Weller has been undoubtedly the driving force behind The Jam, but lead guitarist Paul is not in favour of the star system and would prefer to be recognised as just a member of a band. When they perform live, he refuses to stand in a spotlight, because he does not believe that he deserves more limelight than the others.

Phil Lynott, vocalist, bassist and songwriter for Thin Lizzy hasn't been so bashful: he revels in his role as band leader, and to add to his off-stage playboy image, he plays a silver guitar which he uses during live shows to deflect the spotlights back into the audience.

One leader of the band who served an apprenticeship before he took over his own group is Jeff Lynne, singer, guitarist and song writer of The Electric Light Orchestra. He started his successful career in a 1960s band, The Move, who were led by one of the legends of pop, Roy Wood.

Finally, the exception to prove the rule. One member of an extremely influential band gained more recognition than his group's lead singer, and is still spoken of as the main man in his group. He did write most of their smash hits though, and has a unique guitar playing style. Who is it? Pete Townshend of The Who.

(Left) Richard Jobson.
(Below) Paul Weller.
(Right) Phil Lynott.
(Bottom right) Jeff Lynne.

Gary Numan.

Jimmy Pursey with Sham 69

Bob Geldof with the Boomtown Rats

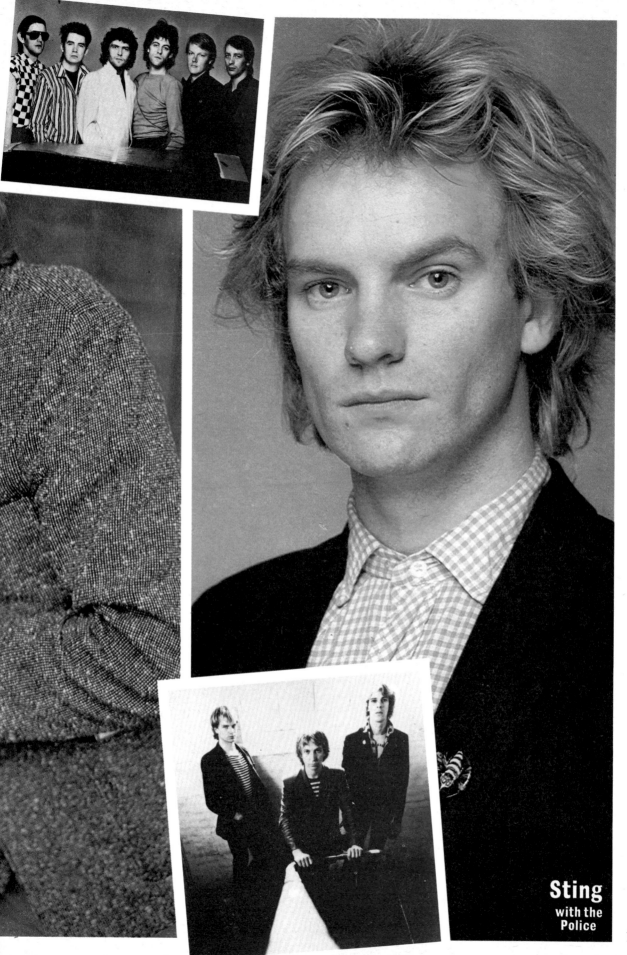

Sting
with the
Police

19

POP QUIZ

1 Who is the lead singer (above) who took his band, The Clash, into the charts earlier this year with *London Calling*?

2 *Tie A Yellow Ribbon* was a no. 1 record back in 1973. Can you remember who recorded it?

3 Pictured below is a negative photograph of a top pop group. Who are they?

5 With which song did Windsor Davies and Don Estelle have a no. 1 record in 1975?

6 ANAGRAM: Rearrange the following letters to give you the name of a famous pop group:
NAT STOWOR MOB

7 The Beatles and Dollar both had a hit record with the same song. What was the song?

9 SLEEVE SPOT: Can you identify this well-known album cover with the give-away lettering deleted?

10 *Eat To The Beat* was a best-selling album for which group?

11 *Leader Of The Gang* and *Rock 'n' Roll* were hits for whom in the mid-'70s?

12 With which form of music would you associate the group Matchbox?

4 *Enough Is Enough* was a hit for two ladies earlier in 1980. Who were they?

8 With which group would you associate Nick Lowe and Dave Edmunds?

20

SPOT THE DIFFERENCE

Above you can see two matching pictures from Thames TV's hilarious comedy series *Robin's Nest*, featuring (left to right) Mr. Nicholls (Tony Britton), Robin (Richard O'Sullivan) and Vicky (Tessa Wyatt). Matching, did we say? Well, not quite. Because the second of the pictures has eight slight alterations. Look closely, and see if you can spot the changes.

The MUPPETS

In the 1976/77 Pye Colour Television Awards the 'Most Promising Male Newcomer' was—a frog! But he's no ordinary swamp-dwelling frog; this one is the producer, director, writer, MC, performer and referee of **The Muppet Show**. And his name, of course, is Kermit.

The award must have been a great honour to Kermit, especially as he spends most of his time frantically waving his spindly arms around in a state of harassment. The reason? Keeping his cast of performers in order is not easy.

There's Fozzie Bear, for instance, the lovable, ear-wiggling comic of the show who tries desperately to be funny and is constantly heckled by Statler and Waldorf from the theatre box.

How to handle a woman? Well, Kermit could do with some advice because the star of his show (so she says) is Miss Piggy, the femme fatale of the animal world.

If these alone aren't enough, there's the Great Gonzo, for whom nothing is too death-defying or ridiculous to achieve superstardom, Robin, Kermit's diminutive but precocious nephew, Rowlf the Dog, who can philosophise about anything that moves, Gladys, the canteen lady who's in constant battle with the Swedish Chef, and, of course, the neanderthal drummer, Animal.

All of these weird and wonderful characters are brought to life by an expert team of puppeteers, under the direction of the Muppets' creator, Jim Henson. They include Frank Oz, Jerry Nelson, Richard Hunt, Dave Goelz and Louise Gold, all performers of such skill that their Muppet charges have become the most widely-known puppet group in the world.

It's A Scarecrow's Life

When Barbara Euphan Todd first set pen to paper to record the exploits of her quarrelsome, sulky but utterly lovable scarecrow, Worzel Gummidge, television was still in its infancy.

There must have been many who missed seeing Miss Todd's splendidly boisterous books, but Worzel's inane caperings were destined to reach a rightfully wider audience when BBC serialised the stories on their famous and long-lamented late afternoon radio programme, **Children's Hour.** Literally overnight, Worzel Gummidge became a

Fireworks all the way when Worzel meets The Crowman (Geoffrey Bayldon).

nationally-known character.

Coincidentally, at roughly the same time, a determined young actor was making his presence felt over the airwaves. His name was Jon Pertwee . . .

Many years were to pass before Jon and Worzel got, so to speak, together. *"I'd always liked Worzel,"* says Jon, *"and being extremely fond of character parts, the more exuberant the better, I realised that I wanted to bring him, visually, to life."*

To convert Barbara Euphan Todd's prose to a script suitable for live action, those two masters of their craft, writers Keith Waterhouse and Willis Hall came together, and the first intention was to produce a cinema film. *"But it was a bad time for British film-making,"* recalls Jon Pertwee. *"It actually took us four years before we persuaded Southern Television to take up the idea as the basis for a small-screen series."*

And so, in 1979, the scarecrow of Scatterbrook Farm stepped into everyone's front room, and the result was an immediate success. Worzel, with his young friends John and Sue, his maker, the Crowman, his haughty and class-conscious ladyfriend, Aunt Sally, and all the assorted locals he pesters to despair, became hot news! Just, indeed, as Jon Pertwee had hoped.

For Jon, it was quite a departure from his previous television role, that of the third **Doctor Who.** He was already internationally known

as the intrepid Tardis-traveller. Did he feel that switching his image so drastically was dangerous? *"Not at all. There was absolutely no similarity between Doctor Who and Worzel Gummidge, after all. I think young people take a character, literally, at face value. None of them would actually have thought it was Doctor Who playing the scarecrow."*

For the record, Jon Pertwee has always managed to bring his characters dramatically to life. RADA trained, he came to the general public's notice in a radio show called **Waterlogged Spa,** starring Eric Barker. Any of your relatives who grew up during the late war years will remember Jon's marvellous portrayal of a comic West Country postman, whose catch phrase was *"What does it matter what you do, as long as you tear 'em up?"* (Incidentally, Worzel himself would be pretty adept at tearing up letters, too. Especially if the act caused the maximum of inconvenience to the villagers of Scatterbrook!)

Jon's acting had already won acclaim in the world of the theatre. No less a person than the late Sir Noel Coward had singled him out for praise. *"That young man will go far,"* the 'Master' once said. An entertainment critic in a national newspaper of April 1951 was even more specific—and possibly blessed with second sight. *"If Jon Pertwee is wise,"* he wrote, *"he will devote his future to television. He has a comedy voice and a brilliant sense of character*

Heads it's Worzel! (Left to right) Singing Head, Butler Head, Thinking Head, and Jolly Uncle Head. (Above) Sue (Charlotte Coleman) and John (Jeremy Austin) join Worzel.

For Better Or Worzel!

ter, and his mobile, elfish face is really funny to look at . . ."

"I hope it is," laughs Jon. "Especially as Worzel, with real mud on it. No, we can't use stage make-up. It just doesn't look right. Oh yes, and Worzel's warts! Do you know what they are? Sugar Puffs cut in half!"

Worzel Gummidge may be adventurous. Nobody could say otherwise, considering a scarecrow capable of wandering hither and thither, changing his heads to suit his needs, nursing a robin in the region of his straw-stuffed belly-button. But it may come as a surprise to know that Jon Pertwee himself leaves the bird-baiting old rag-bag far behind when it comes to a love of action! Believe it or not, Jon was once a wall-of-death rider, one of those heart-stopping characters who rides a motorbike around a circular, *vertical* enclosure. He was also a bare-back rider in a circus. Motorbikes remain one of Jon's obsessions. He rides his own collected machines in veteran runs, and when travelling between his home and location, he prefers two-wheeled transport to anything else. "I was once riding home along the Victoria Embankment," he says, "and I'd pulled up at some traffic lights. Suddenly, another bike coasted up beside me, and the rider raised his goggles, looked across, and said 'fancy a burn-up, then?' I did a swift double-take until I realised it was Sir Ralph Richardson (the world-famous actor), another dedicated biker!"

Jon's also accident prone. He was injured doing a Wild West horseback act in 1960. He broke a leg skiing. He nearly drowned scuba diving, when his airline fouled the anchor of a boat. He narrowly missed sinking a racing car in quicksands while testing it on Southport beach. Another diving incident found him facing a shark which, although much annoyed by another diver prodding it in the backside, somehow decided not to attack. Oh yes, *and* Jon was fallen on by fellow-actor Bernard Bresslaw during the filming of a show. From twenty feet, would you believe! "Bernard is certainly no lightweight," commented Jon wryly from his hospital bed, afterwards!

"Let 'em eat cake!" Worzel and Aunt Sally (Una Stubbs) believe whole-heartedly in the phrase.

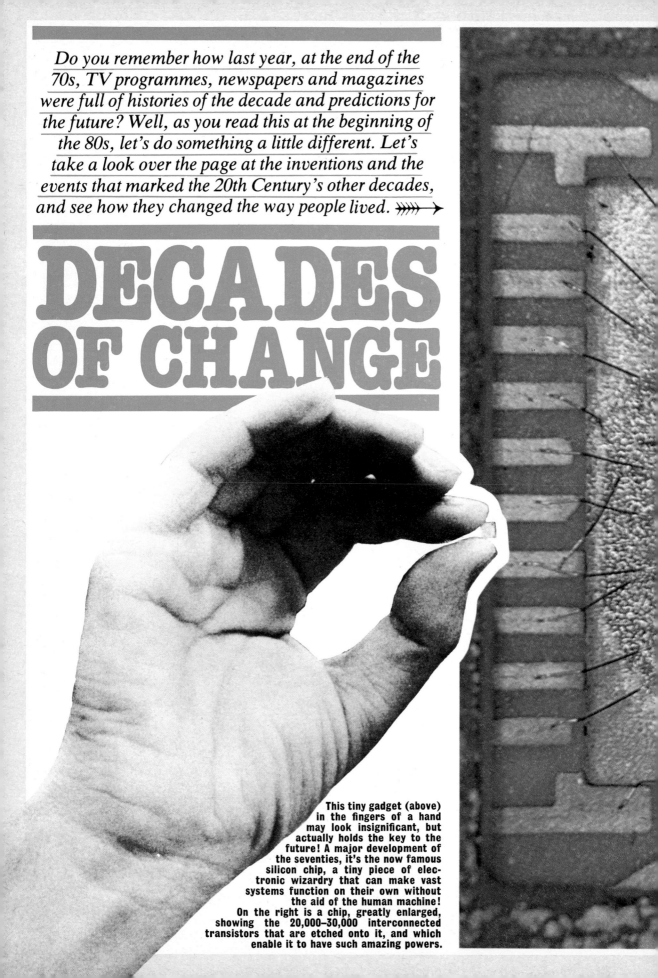

Do you remember how last year, at the end of the 70s, TV programmes, newspapers and magazines were full of histories of the decade and predictions for the future? Well, as you read this at the beginning of the 80s, let's do something a little different. Let's take a look over the page at the inventions and the events that marked the 20th Century's other decades, and see how they changed the way people lived. ⇛→

DECADES
OF CHANGE

This tiny gadget (above) in the fingers of a hand may look insignificant, but actually holds the key to the future! A major development of the seventies, it's the now famous silicon chip, a tiny piece of electronic wizardry that can make vast systems function on their own without the aid of the human machine! On the right is a chip, greatly enlarged, showing the 20,000–30,000 interconnected transistors that are etched onto it, and which enable it to have such amazing powers.

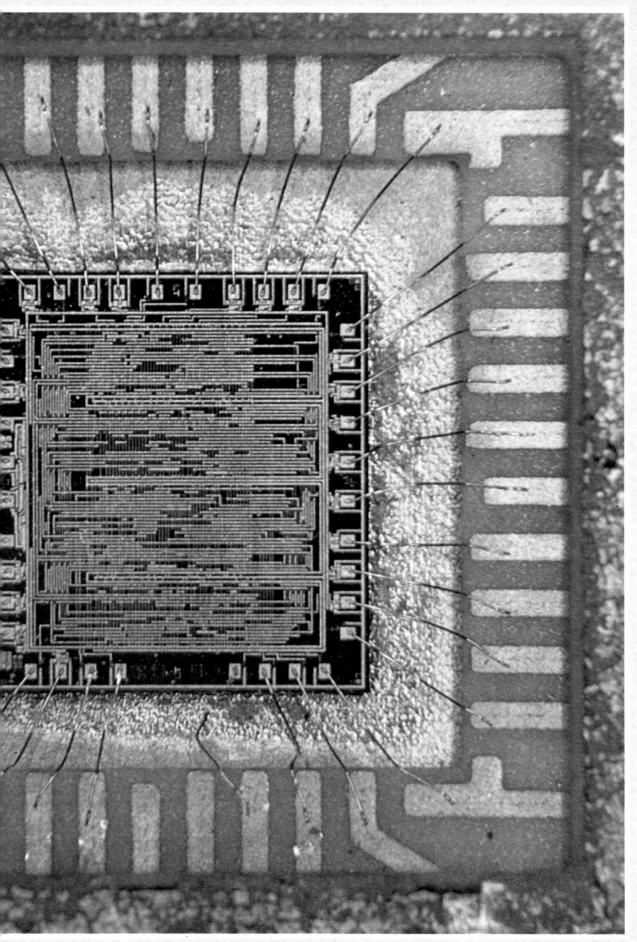

1900s

This was the decade which saw the most important car ever built, the Model T Ford (**below**). It was the first mass-produced automobile and its price actually went down, from £150 to £125 in its first five years. The Model T scared the living daylights out of horse and buggy drivers. They thought the world would change with so many of these little motors buzzing around. They were right.

Almost as mighty an impact was created by an experiment carried out by a Mr Marconi. He sat in Newfoundland fiddling with a mass of wires and valves, and he received a noise all the way from Cornwall. Eureka! The Radio was invented. That, too, really did change world history.

Bare faced horror on the streets! King Gillette invented his safety razor with the disposable blade. Suddenly men began to lose their bushy moustaches and beards.

Meanwhile other things were taking off. In 1903 Wilbur and Orville Wright made the first powered, controlled and sustained flight near Kitty Hawk, USA.

Other flying objects were hitting the ground in huge numbers in that year. Aerosols, using carbon dioxide as a propellant, were introduced, but it wasn't until the mid-40s that they were used in large quantities, when American troops were issued with insect sprays for jungle campaigns.

1910s

This decade started brightly, for in 1910 colour photography was introduced. Used mostly in America, Germany and Austria at first it was to change the look of books and magazines forever.

Bleep-dip, Bleep-dip, Bleep-dip. Not a Martian landing, but a sound invented by the French. The 'Asdic' method of tracking submarines. It was used in the Great War of 1914–18 when the Allies feared that their fleets would be blown from the waters by German U-boats, but Asdic changed the balance of the war at sea. More wartime horrors. This time the British invented something—it was in Cambrai, France, that the first tank was seen in action. That, too, altered centuries of military tactics, and people even thought it would end wars for ever.

But one invention in 1914 did not prove a let down. Mary Jacob invented a brassiere which has been the basis of modern designs ever since. And you could fetch it home nice and clean from the shop, too, for Jacques Brandenberg, a French Dye chemist, had seen through a particular wrapping paper problem, so he invented Cellophane clear wrapping. Meanwhile Gedeon Sunback of America was dressing and undressing easier. He invented the zip fastener in 1915.

But the century's second decade will be remembered with mixed feelings, most of all because 1914 was the year of the Russian Revolution. That was the start of modern-day Communism, the greatest social change in recent world history.

1920s

You don't have to be a genius to appreciate the impact of an invention launched in 1924. John Logie Baird (**below**) introduced the first system for television, developed in a lab near Dorking. Unfortunately it

was not capable of refinement for widespread transmissions, so another system was used. Television changed the world, and has educated and informed over half-a-century of development.

People certainly made a big effort to seem happy in the 1920s. It was the decade of the Flapper, those thrill-seekers who danced the Charleston and the Bunny Hop through the night (they couldn't say they didn't know what time it was because their watch had stopped—John Harwood invented the self-winding watch in 1924). People flocked to the cinema in their millions all round the world. New heroes were established, new standards of behaviour and beauty were portrayed. The movies were responsible for another huge change in people's lives and ambitions. But while films remained silent for several years, ears pricked up at the announcement of another great institution. BBC Radio started in 1922 and earned a reputation, which it still holds, as the best of its kind in the world. Why, you can count its rivals on earth on the fingers of one hand. And talking of fingers, another hiccough in the world's eating habits occurred ·in 1927. A momentous discovery: fish fingers arrived!

1930s

Not a particularly happy 10 years, at least the latter part. The Nazis started marching into other people's countries, and it didn't end in a few months as many experts predicted. In fact, the World still hasn't fully recovered from the Second World War.

But it wasn't all doom and gloom. The end of the 'twenties had seen a huge economic slump, the worst the world had known. It was supposed to have resulted in famine, more wars, revolutions and vast poverty. But somehow people staggered through the 1930s having lots of fun, so maybe they hadn't read the newspapers properly. It was a flashy decade, in more ways than one—the flash bulb was invented in 1930, so lots more nighttime and indoor pictures appeared, mostly of people squinting their eyes. And as huge business corporations crashed in the Slump, other empires were built up when the world's most successful board game, *Monopoly*, was invented, in 1936. Stockings became cheaper and sheerer

when nylon was introduced in 1937, leading to a revolution in fashion. Now the poorer classes could dress in the latest 'threads'. Other ups and downs included the invention of the modern helicopter (**above**) in 1930. It was supposed to replace the winged aircraft and eventually replace buses and trains in cities. Another far-reaching invention, also in the air, was Frank Whittle's Jet Engine but it wasn't developed well enough to play a full part in the War. And the BBC were at it in the 30s too, when they started the world's first regular television service in 1936

1940s

The War was at its height now. But it wasn't a totally awful decade. Anticipating peace, someone invented the modern Colour television set. And there was a giant step towards wiping out many terrible diseases, when Penicillin was introduced in a big way, thanks to Sir Alexander Fleming's (below) work. Radar was perfected in the mid-40s too, enabling future generations to enjoy a sophisticated world air transport system, not to mention its limitless other benefits. And as the radar screen became more widespread, so did the cinema screen. Cinerama was invented in 1940, a huge movie screen brought into action in the

1950s to lure people away from television. But bigger didn't mean better—it didn't succeed until the films they showed on it improved.

This was the era when everyone's ideas on writing began to change. The invention by Mr Waterman in 1884 of the Fountain Pen was overtaken by a Mr Biro (below) in 1944 when he introduced the ball-point pen. They advertised it as 'the pen that writes under water' but as deep sea divers wait till they surface before writing home, that didn't make a lot of sense.

1950s

You could hear all the latest news wherever you were after 1953 when the transistor was invented, enabling portable radios (above) to shrink in size and weight. It had a far reaching effect on the entire electronics industry, too. Meanwhile, jet technology was speeding ahead, and Britain was in the lead. The world's first turbo-jet airliner, the Comet, made the world's inaugural jet passenger service flight to Johannesburg in South Africa in 1952. The experts called it 'the world shrinker' and for once they were right. To shrink it further still, by taking lumps out of it, the British exploded their first atom bomb in that year too. It scared a lot of

people, and protest marches took place around the country. The 50s made protest marches very popular, though whether they actually achieved anything is in doubt. What is sure is that a few blisters could have been saved if they waited till later in the decade for Alec Issigonis (above) to invent the Mini. A cheap car (less than £500 then) which not only revolutionised car design but also introduced a new word into the language.

1960s

And mini was to mean a lot more, or rather a lot less, in the 60s. They were the 'Swinging 60s' and one thing that made them so was the mini skirt. British designer Mary Quant was credited with their introduction. She was part of a new British revival in the popular fields of music (The Beatles [below] & Co), films, night life, photography and generally enjoying yourself.

A fast-moving idea, which hovered in the air, rather than forged ahead, to "alter transport as we knew it," (as the experts again predicted wrongly) was the invention of the Hovercraft by Christopher Cockerell. Experts and ordinary folk alike, still can't understand why it hasn't fulfilled its early promise. Maybe people's hearts weren't in it.

Actually, where people's hearts were, became a sensation of the 60s. In South Africa in 1967 Dr Christian Barnard performed the first successful heart transplant. Well, quite successful, his patient survived for 18 days. But 'replacement' surgery became a reality from that day, and really did transform world medicine.

While beyond the world itself, Neil Armstrong created cosmic history in 1969 by becoming the first man ever to set foot on the moon. Space travel had achieved an incredible goal, and could rightly claim to be this century's most awe-inspiring development.

1970s

Technology was really taking hold when the 70s dawned. It was the decade of the world's first commercial supersonic passenger aircraft, the Concorde (below). Trains got quicker too; in Britain they put paid to the old British Rail 'lumbering' image, with 125mph journeys, rivalling travel times of jet plane services. The silicon chip was developed, allowing whole factories to be taken over by machines—without a

human in sight! The 70s also saw startling, not to say frightening, advances in discoveries about the human body. DNA, the 'units of heredity', were coming under scientists' power. They discovered that the units that made up the human organism could be altered. In other words people could soon be built to order, with whatever physical and mental characteristics their makers desired. So it could be that the most revolutionary and dramatic change in world history will happen not in the machines and inventions around us, but in the human race itself. Let's hope the 1980s is a decade of good sense. We have so much power now—anything can happen . . .

The SMURFS

It has only taken a couple of years for those funny little characters that we call **Smurfs** to establish themselves as some of this country's favourite novelties.

It all started one evening when a Belgian artist, Pierre Culliford, was having a meal. He asked somebody to pass the salt, but used the Flemish equivalent of thingummybob—'Schtroumpfe'. He then decided that that was just the name he had been searching for to call a gang of dwarves he was drawing for a cartoon.

Schtroumpfes developed into children's books and annuals in Belgium and soon spread into other Continental countries. That was thirty years ago!

Pierre could not have realised that night what he was about to unleash on the unsuspecting world. The ensuing years have seen a whole host of smurfenalia spring up in our high-street shops.

The Smurfs have also been one of the most unusual groups ever to have grabbed the attention of record-buyers with hit singles like **Smurf Song** and **Dippetty Day.**

Accompanying them on their early records was a man called Pierre Kartner, better known to us as **Father Abraham.** At the age of eight, after winning a local singing competition, he decided that singing was to be his future. His first professional success came towards the end of 1969 when he wrote most of the songs for, and produced, an album for a group called **Corry and the Rekels,** which became an enormous hit in his homeland. As a singer in his own right, Pierre recorded over 40 hit singles and 10 top-selling albums from 1970 onwards.

The Smurfs: © S.E.P.P. and Peyo Belgium

31

LAUGH-IN

Q) Why does a bald-headed man have no use for keys?
A) *Because he has lost his locks.*

Q) Who tells chicken jokes?
A) *Comedihens.*
Q) What do ghosts have for breakfast?
A) *Dreaded wheat.*

Customer:
I'd like some poison for mice.
Chemist:
Have you tried Boots?
Customer: I want to poison them —not kick them to death.

Customer:
Will the band play anything I request?
Waiter: Certainly, sir.
Customer:
Tell them to play cards.

Barber:
Were you wearing a red scarf when you came in?
Customer: No.
Barber: Oh! Then I must have cut your throat.

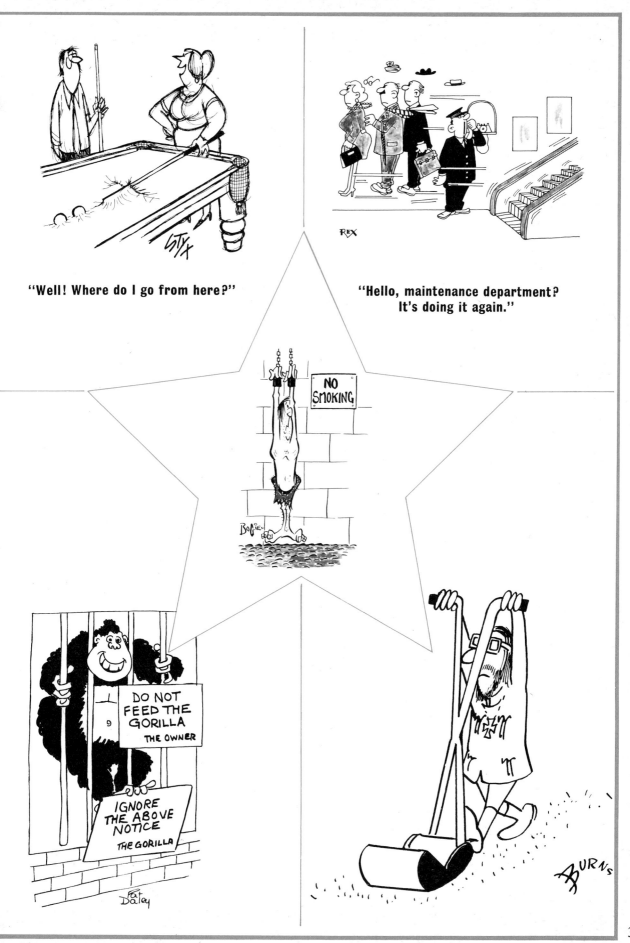

"Well! Where do I go from here?"

"Hello, maintenance department? It's doing it again."

ABBA
THE EARLY YEARS

In past years, we've had *ABBA—The Movie* and *ABBA—The Album*. We've even had *ABBA—The Soap!* Later on in this annual you can try your hand at *ABBA— The Quiz*. But in this special picture-strip section, let's concentrate on *ABBA—The Story*, based on some of the material which first appeared in Look-in during 1977 . . .

ABBA — THE QUARTET THAT HAS DOMINATED THE WORLD OF POP SINCE THE MID-SEVENTIES. FOUR CHARACTERS, EACH WITH A VERY DIFFERENT TALE TO TELL ABOUT THE EARLY YEARS. TAKE ANNI-FRID 'FRIDA' LYNGSTAD, FOR INSTANCE...

YOU KNOW, I'M THE OLDEST MEMBER OF ABBA. AND I'M NOT REALLY SWEDISH. I WAS BORN IN NORWAY, THIRTY FOUR YEARS AGO, IN A VILLAGE NEAR NARVIK. MY FATHER WAS A GERMAN OFFICER...

"IN THAT PART OF NORWAY, THE GERMAN INVADERS WERE HATED. SO, AT THE END OF THE WAR, MY GRANDMOTHER TOOK ME TO SWEDEN..."

"I GREW UP IN HARDSHIP. MY GRANDMOTHER HAD TO WORK LONG HOURS, JUST TO SURVIVE. FOR ME, THE ONLY PLEASURE WAS IN OUR GRAMOPHONE, AND THE JAZZ RECORDS, WE HAD.."

IT'S ONLY FOR THE OLD SEVENTY-EIGHTS! NOT FOR THE RECORDS **WE** MAKE, STIG!

AH! THEY'RE PLAYED ON THE LATEST EQUIPMENT, FRIDA! BUT TELL THEM HOW YOU STARTED SINGING. WHAT WERE YOU? ELEVEN YEARS OLD...?

OUR MANAGER STIG ANDERSON HAS JUST SUCH A GRAMOPHONE IN HIS OFFICE TODAY. IT OFTEN REMINDS ME OF MY YOUTH...

YES. I WAS ELEVEN WHEN I MADE MY FIRST PUBLIC APPEARANCE. AT A RED CROSS BAZAAR. THE NUMBER I SANG WAS RATHER JAZZY — FOR I'VE ALWAYS BEEN KEEN ON JAZZ MUSIC...

BY THE TIME I WAS THIRTEEN, I WAS SINGING REGULARLY WITH A SWINGY DANCE BAND LED BY A MAN CALLED EWALD EK..."

SHE'S NOT HALF BAD! REMINDS ME A BIT OF PEGGY LEE...

"YES, WELL, PEGGY LEE WAS ONE OF MY IDOLS. STILL IS. YOU KNOW I ACTUALLY MET HER ON ABBA'S FIRST VISIT TO AMERICA IN 1974...?"

BUT I'M JUMPING AHEAD! IT WAS MY AMBITION TO BE LIKE PEGGY LEE, ELLA FITZGERALD, SARAH VAUGHAN, THAT MADE ME MOVE TO THE BIG BAND SCENE. I SANG WITH BENGT SANDLUND'S OUTFIT IN A PLACE CALLED ESKILSTUNA...

IT WAS THERE THAT ANNI-FRID MET A PART-TIME MUSICIAN NAMED RAGNAR FREDRIKSSON, AND MARRIED HIM. WITH TWO CHILDREN COMING ALONG—HANS AND LISE-LOTTE—SHE MIGHT HAVE SETTLED INTO A HOUSEWIFE ROUTINE...

IN FACT, SHE KEPT GOING WITH A SMALL GROUP RAGNAR ORGANISED FOR HER. THEY GOT LOTS OF LOCAL WORK...

AND SHE WAS STUDYING SINGING, AND ENTERING ALL SORTS OF TALENT COMPETITIONS! IT WAS TOO MUCH, FRIDA, RIGHT?

OH, YES. SOMETHING HAD TO GIVE. IT WAS INEVITABLE THAT THE MARRIAGE BROKE UP. BUT IT WAS A FRIENDLY PARTING...

IT WAS IN 1967 THAT FRIDA GOT THE BIG BREAK. A NATIONAL TALENT CONTEST, A SWEDISH VERSION OF 'NEW FACES', IF YOU LIKE. IN STOCKHOLM'S FAMOUS SKANSEN PARK...

AND FIRST IN THE SOLO CLASS— ANNI-FRID LYNGSTAD! A BIG HAND FOR FRIDA, EVERYONE!

WHAT ARE YOUR PLANS NOW, FRIDA?

OOOH! JUST GO HOME TO ESKILSTUNA AND **SLEEP!** IT'S ALL **WONDERFUL**, BUT I'M ABSOLUTELY WORN OUT!

OH NO SHE WON'T FOLKS! THE WINNER GETS DRIVEN DIRECTLY TO THE STUDIOS TO APPEAR ON—YES, THE LENNART HYLAND TELEVISION SHOW!

STIG ANDERSON, ABBA'S LIVE-WIRE BOSS, REMEMBERED THE OCCASION WELL!

POOR FRIDA WAS SHATTERED! BUT IN FACT, IT WAS AN ENORMOUS PIECE OF LUCK. THE DAY WAS SEPTEMBER 3, 1967—THE DAY SWEDEN CHANGED OVER FROM DRIVING ON THE LEFT TO DRIVING ON THE RIGHT!

"SO LENNART HYLAND HAD ORGANISED A HUGE ARRAY OF TALENT DESIGNED TO KEEP PEOPLE OFF THE ROADS, AND IN FRONT OF THEIR TELEVISION SETS..."

CUE ANNI-FRID LYNGSTAD!

37

39

TOUGH LUCK, BJORN. BUT YOU MUST'VE KNOWN IT WAS COMING, SOONER OR LATER.

THAT'S NO COMFORT. AND IT'S OKAY FOR YOU, HANSI. YOU'RE A GERMAN CITIZEN. YOU DON'T COME UNDER OUR SWEDISH LAWS.

ACTUALLY, WE MANAGED TO WANGLE DEFERMENTS. AND OUR FOLK-BASED QUARTET WENT ON FROM STRENGTH TO STRENGTH.

"WE TOURED EXTENSIVELY IN THE PUBLIC PARKS..."

"WE HAD A SERIES OF SIX TELEVISION SHOWS IN GERMANY..."

I ALWAYS SAY THESE AMERICAN GROUPS ARE THE BEST, KLAUS!

AMERICAN? WHY, THEY'RE **SWEDISH.** YOU DUMMY!

THEY MADE RECORDS. AND AS ABBA CHIEF STIG ANDERSON NOW RECALLS...

WE RELEASED THEM IN BRITAIN AND AMERICA, BUT UNDER THE NAME OF 'THE NORTHERN LIGHTS'. WE DIDN'T FEEL THAT 'HOOTENANNY' SOUNDED RIGHT.

AND THE DISCS WENT JUST LIKE A LEAD BALLOON! KER-PLUNK!

HUH! **WE** MADE THE CHARTS, BENNY!

UMM. BUT ONLY IN SOUTH AFRICA, I'M AFRAID!

WHAT A SIGHT! WHAT WOULD OUR FANS HAVE SAID IF WE'D ROLLED OUT ON STAGE LIKE THIS!

NEVER MIND FANS ANY MORE. IT'S THE SERGEANT MAJORS WE'RE GOING TO HAVE TO IMPRESS!

WELL, ANYWAY! AT LAST THE MILITARY **DID** CATCH UP WITH US. TONY, JOHAN AND I WERE ORDERED TO REPORT TO THE LIFEGUARDS DEPOT FOURTEEN, AT LINKOPING...

BUT THE COMMANDER AT DEPOT FOURTEEN WAS ASTONISHINGLY BROADMINDED!

WE'RE GRANTING YOU SPECIAL REGULAR LEAVE. NIGHTS AND WEEKENDS SO THAT YOU CAN CONTINUE AS A GROUP.

THAT'S WONDERFUL, SIR! WE'D RESIGNED OURSELVES TO BREAKING UP!

BUT I'M A FAN OF YOURS! AND I SUPPOSE THE BRIGADE COMMANDER MUST BE, TOO!

COME ON! LET'S PHONE HANSI AND TELL HIM THE GOOD NEWS!

THEIR ARMY SERVICE OVER, THEY WERE STILL A SUCCESS. BJORN, DETERMINED TO STUDY BUSINESS ECONOMICS AND LAW, TOOK ON A JOB WITH STIG ANDERSON AT POLAR MUSIC...

YOU'LL WEAR YOURSELF OUT, YOUNG MAN! WORKING HERE ALL DAY, SINGING NIGHTS ...AND WRITING MUSIC WHENEVER YOU'VE GOT A MOMENT! DON'T YOU SLEEP?

WHAT'S 'SLEEP'..?

BY 1968, I'D BEGAN RECORDING SOLO, APART FROM DISCS WITH THE HOOTENANNYS. I DID A SWEDISH VERSION OF BOBBY GOLDSBORO'S HIT, 'HONEY'...

THAT, AND 'FROKEN FREDRIKSSON'— OTHERWISE JEANNIE C. RILEY'S 'HARPER VALLEY P.T.A.' PUT BJORN IN THE SCANDINAVIAN HIT PARADES. AND SOON, INEVITABLY, THE HOOTENANNY SINGERS WERE TO BREAK UP...

SO IF YOU'D BEEN IN SWEDEN IN THE SUMMER OF 1969, YOU MIGHT HAVE SEEN BJORN ULVAEUS PERFORMING A SONG ON A TELEVISION POP SHOW. YOU'D HAVE SEEN HIM SING 'TANGOKAVALJEREN' AND SEEN HIM DANCE THE TANGO AS WELL...

I MIGHT HAVE WORRIED ABOUT SPLITTING MY TROUSERS... IF MY MIND HADN'T BEEN ON A SUPER LOOKING BLONDE SINGER WHO WAS ALSO ON THE SHOW!

IT WAS AGNETHA FALTSKOG –NOW ONE OF BJORN'S SCINTILLATING COLLEAGUES IN ABBA!

WHEW! I'VE GOT TO GET TO KNOW HER BETTER!

THEY HAD MET A FEW TIMES BEFORE... BUT NOW THE ROMANCE TOOK OFF, THE NEWSPAPERS CALLED IT 'THE LOVE STORY OF THE YEAR'..!

WE'VE BEEN RECOGNISED! ARE YOU EMBARRASSED..?

ARE YOU...?

NOT WHEN I CONSIDER THE PUBLICITY! HI, THERE!

OH! ER WE DIDN'T MEAN TO STARE...

OKAY, OKAY! IT WASN'T THE **ELASTIC** THAT NEEDED MORE STRENGTH, BUT **ME**...!

FOR AFTER LEAVING HIGH SCHOOL, AGNETHA TOOK A JOB AS A TELEPHONIST...

HELLO, CAN I HELP YOU? LONG-DISTANCE TO NORWAY? CERTAINLY SIR!

AND IN THE EVENINGS SHE WAS SINGING WITH BENGT ENGHART'S ORCHESTRA FROM HUSQVARNA...

WE DID A LOT OF TOURING – AND SOMETIMES I WOULDN'T GET HOME UNTIL FIVE IN THE MORNING. SINCE I HAD TO BE AT THE SWITCHBOARD AT EIGHT, IT WAS TERRIBLY HARD GOING!

SHE HAD TO MAKE A CHOICE - AND HER DECISION DIDN'T EXACTLY MEET WITH FAMILY ENTHUSIASM!

HONESTLY, AGNETHA! DO YOU THINK YOU CAN MAKE A LIVING AS A SINGER?

IT'S ALL VERY WELL TO HAVE IT AS A HOBBY, BUT AS A **CAREER**...?

BENGT ENGHARDT'S ORCHESTRA MADE THE RECORD... AND IT WAS SUBMITTED TO A PRODUCER OF CBS/CUPOL...AN EX-ROCK STAR CALLED LITTLE GERHARD...

THE BREAK CAME WITH THE FIRST RECORD. AGNETHA HAD WRITTEN A SONG - JAG VAR SÅ KÄR –'SO MUCH IN LOVE'...

OKAY, EVERYONE. WE'LL PROBABLY HAVE TO DO SEVERAL TAKES FOR YOUR DEMO TAPE. JUST RELAX– AND FORGET YOU'RE IN A STUDIO!

THE EVENTUAL RELEASE, AGNETHA BACKED BY SVEN-OLOFF WALLDOFF'S ORCHESTRA, SMASHED INTO THE SWEDISH CHARTS. IT WAS AN INCREDIBLE SUCCESS...

FATHER? I'VE MADE NUMBER THREE! ISN'T IT FABULOUS?

HEY, YOU'VE NO IDEA HOW EMBARRASSING IT WAS! HE LIKED THE SONG, HE LIKED MY VOICE BUT HE DIDN'T LIKE THE ORCHESTRA!

THAT'S THE WAY IT SOMETIMES GOES! SO THEY ASKED YOU IN TO RE-MAKE THE NUMBER ALONE!

BJORN ULVAEUS HAD ALREADY MET AGNETHA SEVERAL TIMES. THEY GOT ON WELL, BUT AS HE EXPLAINS...

I DIDN'T SEE ANY FUTURE FOR **US**. AGNETHA HAD BECOME ENGAGED TO A GERMAN COMPOSER AND RECORD PRODUCER - DIETER ZIMMERMAN. HE HAD PROMISED TO PUT HER OVER BIG IN HIS OWN COUNTRY!

IN FACT, IT WAS A DISASTER! DISCOURAGED FROM USING HER OWN MATERIAL, AGNETHA HAD TO SING GERMAN SONGS. ALL WERE FLOPS...

DON'T SEE MUCH OF AGNETHA FALTSKOG IN THE CHARTS THESE DAYS!

OH! SHE'LL BE BACK. THEY SAY SHE'S GOT A NEW SWEDISH RECORD COMING OUT SHORTLY!

IT CAME OUT — ZIGNENARVAN — 'GIPSY FRIEND.' JUST AT THE SAME TIME AS A RED-HOT CONTROVERSY BROKE IN THE SWEDISH PRESS ABOUT GIPSIES IN THE COUNTRY! GOOD PUBLICITY? NO WAY!

THE PAPERS TORE HER TO BITS! ACCUSED HER OF 'TASTELESS EXPLOITATION' AND SHE'D ONLY WRITTEN THE MUSIC, NOT THE LYRICS!

MORE THAN THAT! THE SONG HAD BEEN WRITTEN LONG BEFORE THE GIPSY TROUBLE! BUT NOBODY WOULD BELIEVE IT!

LIKE ALL THINGS, HOWEVER, IT BLEW OVER, IT WAS REPLACED BY ANOTHER PROBLEMATIC NUMBER!

OM TARAR VORE GULD...

OM TARAR VORE GULD. 'IF TEARS WERE GOLD.' AS AGNETHA TOLD THE PRESS AT THE TIME — "IT'S FANTASTIC! WHEN I SING IT, PEOPLE BEGIN TO KISS EACH OTHER!"

OHHHH! IT MAKES ME FEEL — AS IF I'M MELTING...

BUT THERE WAS A PROBLEM. A DANISH COMPOSER, PER HVIID CLAIMED THE SONG WAS HIS. HE SAID HE TOURED SWEDEN IN 1950, AND PLAYED THE TUNE. SAYING TH I NOTED IT DOWN ONLY ONE THING — I WAS **BORN** IN 1950...!

SO THAT'S AGNETHA'S STORY. SOON AFTER THAT, ALL FOUR OF US GOT TOGETHER AS A RECORDING GROUP...

IT'S NAME? WELL IF YOU TAKE **A** FOR AGNETHA, **B** FOR BENNY, **B** FOR BJORN AND **A** FOR ANNI-FRID, WHAT HAVE YOU GOT? **ABBA**! BUT THEN, THAT'S ANOTHER STORY...!

ABBA — THE QUIZ

Just how much do you know about that ABBA story? Here's your chance to find out, as we test your knowledge of what happened after the famous foursome teamed up . . .

(1) Their first huge hit in Britain was a Eurovision Song Contest winner. What was its title?

(2) At the beginning of the Year Of The Child in 1979, they donated all royalties from a particular hit to UNICEF. What was that hit?

(3) In *ABBA—The Movie* from 1978, the story and concert scenes take place in which country?

(4) Complete these song titles:
D – – C – – – – UE – –
– O – – Y – – R – OT – E – K – O –?
– – RN – – D –

(5) Agnetha and Bjorn were divorced last year. How many children have they?

(6) What instrument(s) does Benny usually play?

(7) What record label do ABBA appear on in Britain?

(8) One of their album covers featured a photograph of a helicopter. Which one?

(9) From which hit song do these words come: "Half past twelve and I'm watchin' the late show"?

(10) And finally: cast your mind back to last Christmas (1979). What was ABBA's huge hit then?

ANSWERS

1. Waterloo; 2. Chiquitita; 3. Australia; 4. Dancing Queen, Does Your Mother Know; 5. Two: Linda and Christian; 6. Piano/keyboards; 7. Epic; 8. Arrival; 9. Gimme, Gimme, Gimme (A Man After Midnight); 10. I Have A Dream.

"Woof-woof!"

Patient: Doctor, doctor, I keep thinking I'm a dustbin.
Doctor: Don't talk rubbish.

LAUGH-IN

1st boy: I always tell my mum any bad news when Crossroads is on.
2nd boy: Why?
1st boy: Then all she says is "Shhhh!"

★★★★★★★★★

(Q) Do you need training to be a litter collector?
(A) No, you just pick it up as you go along.

★★★★★★★★★

Waiter: How did you find your steak, sir?
Diner: Easy— I'm a detective.

"Henry, I think you've set the blades too low!"

"I'm a motor mechanic."

"Prisoner in the dock . . ."

Patient: I've got this strange feeling that I'm a bell.
Doctor: Well, if you're not better in a few days, give me a ring.

★★★★★★★★★★

(Q) What goes cluck, cluck, bang?
(A) A chicken in a minefield.

★★★★★★★★★★

(Q) What happens to ducks who fly upside down?
(A) They quack up.

★★★★★★★★★★

Diner: This restaurant must have a very clean kitchen.
Waiter: Thank you, sir, but how did you know?
Diner: Everything tastes of soap.

★★★★★★★★★★

BJ AND THE BEAR

BJ And The Bear has undoubtedly been one of the liveliest series to reach our shores recently.

The show stars 6ft. plus ex-rock star Greg Evigan and, of course, Sam the mischievous chimpanzee. Although Greg was a big hit with the female viewers it was Sam, probably the hairiest star in Hollywood, who really stole the show.

Though this was his first starring role it was by no means his first experience in front of the cameras, for he's appeared in lots of commercials and TV shows in America, including **Fantasy Island.**

For the first series of **BJ And The Bear,** Sam even had a stand-in called Oopsy. Unfortunately Chimp No. 2. was given the sack by Universal Studios for bad behaviour. Apparently, Oopsy became so star-struck and temperamental that in the end he just had to go!

Before getting his big break as BJ, Greg Evigan's acting experience came mostly from the theatre where he once starred in the lead role of Danny Zuko in the Broadway hit musical **Grease.** A certain John Travolta appeared way down the cast list!

In the series Greg plays Billy Joe McKay, an independent man who's survived the horrors of a prison camp in Vietnam to return to his native land with a longing for freedom. Consequently, the life he chooses is that of a free-wheeling truck driver who will haul anything for the right price, and in so doing gets involved in some pretty hairy (sorry Sam) adventures.

Altogether, **BJ And The Bear** has brought a whole new meaning to that old showbiz expression 'a double-act'!

GREAT BRITONS

British athletics achieved much in the 1950s but the triumph that really captured the public's imagination was the smashing of the four-minute barrier for the mile, the 'blue-riband' event of running.

In the rather unlikely setting of the Iffley Road track in Oxford, with the aid of Chris Chataway and Chris Brasher, who shared pacemaking duties, the willowy figure of Roger Bannister broke the barrier that had become known as the "Everest" of athletics.

Almost before the cheering had died down, just seven weeks later, Australian John Landy ran even faster in a special race staged in Finland. However, all the glory went to Bannister as the first man to achieve the "impossible".

Without the aid of Chris Brasher (above) and Chris Chataway, Bannister could never have made his successful effort. Both Brasher and Chataway went on to individual successes later in their careers.

(Right) Brasher, Bannister, Stampfl and Chataway discuss their record-breaking race. The winning lap times that day were 57.5, 60.7, 62.3 and 58.9 sec., adding up to 3 min. 59.4 seconds.

GOLDEN GIRL MARY

Great Britain earned an amazing double victory in the 1964 Tokyo Olympics when both Mary Rand and Lynn Davies leapt for gold in the long jump event. Shortly before her victory, Mary gave an interview to the press in which she said that she would like to establish a new world record for the women's long jump in the Olympics. This she did with a jump of 22ft. 2¼in. Mary collected a full set of medals by coming runner-up in the pentathlon and gaining a bronze in the 4 by 100 metres relay. In capturing the men's event Lynn Davies managed a magnificent 26ft. 5¾ins.

With all the goings-on during the summer, British athletics has come in for a lot of attention this year, hasn't it? You can read over the page about a couple of our newest record breakers. But take a look here at what could come as a bit of a surprise: a reminder of some of Britain's great athletic achievements in the past. And there are more of them than you might think . . .

MARATHON MAN

Jim Peters will always be remembered for the race he didn't win! In the Commonwealth Games in Vancouver in 1954 he entered the stadium 15 minutes ahead of the second-placed man. But Peters never made it to the finishing line. Rolling from side to side, falling to the ground and crawling along on all fours, he was finally led from the track and taken to hospital. He was later

awarded a specially struck gold medal from the Duke of Edinburgh which read: "To J. Peters as a token of admiration for a most gallant marathon runner". Jim Peters never won an Olympic medal but he consistently lowered the world record for the marathon. He brought new discipline to the event in the early 1950s, reigning supreme in all the major events bar the Olympics. Between 1952 and 1954 he lowered the world record from 2 hr. 16 min. 7 sec. to 2 hr. 17 min. 39.4 sec., a wonderful achievement.

BATTLING BRASHER

This is the story of a man who would be the first to admit that he was no super-athlete. Yet he achieved Gold where others, who smashed world records, won nothing when it came to the Olympics. For many years Chris Brasher was just another average middle-distance man, best known as Roger Bannister's pacemaker and companion in training. Then he switched to steeplechase. The times slowly improved. In the 1952 Olympics he ran 11th out of 12 after hurting himself early in the race. Four years later he was off to Australia, still very much our second string, to John Disley. All that changed in the final where Chris ran a new Olympic and U.K. record time of 8 min. 41.2 sec. to win gold. He almost saw the victory snatched from his grasp for at first he was disqualified for alleged obstruction but was later reinstated. Chris Brasher's victory should serve as a lesson to all athletes who think that they will never make it to the top.

HEMERY'S HURDLES

Although David Hemery won the 400 metres hurdles for Great Britain, in the 1968 Mexico Olympics, he'd done most of his training in the United States. The '68 games has become known as the 'high altitude Games' and this factor influenced many of the winning times. Not Hemery's—he won his event by a staggering margin of seven yards, in an Olympic and World record time of 48.1 seconds.

Sebastian Coe

It was over just two months in the summer of last year that the name Sebastian Coe thrust itself into sporting history and created an impact never to be forgotten.

Sebastian, 22 at the time, took three incredible athletic track world titles—the first man ever to achieve this feat. The 800 metres, the mile and the 1500 metres records were all shattered within six amazing weeks, and no-one—originally at least—was more surprised than Sheffield-born Seb. He recalls his most publicised record-breaking event, the one mile: *"I had gone to Oslo determined to do well, but there was no intention of aiming for the world record. Everything just happened on the night. I was completely relaxed and not nervous at all and that's what made the difference.*

There was something not quite real about it, because apart from an Olympic gold medal the world record is what every athlete dreams of . . .'

Photograph by Steve Hale

Steve Ovett

Last year Brighton's Steve Ovett came within a whisker of Seb Coe's 1,500 metres world record with a stirring performance in Brussels—he failed that time by a mere eight hundredths of a second. He also clocked 3 min. 49.6 seconds for the mile, (then the best-ever in Britain), but was still three-fifths of a second slower than Seb's 1979 record.

Ovett has a superb athletic pedigree. He won a European Junior Championships gold medal in 1973, found victory in the European Cup, succeeded in the 1977 World Cup, and in 1978 won gold (1,500 metres) and silver (800 metres) medals in the European Championships.

His coach Harry Wilson sums up: *"Sometimes he can't understand why running and racing comes so easily to him when others have to struggle to achieve less. He has felt from the very beginning of his athletics career that he had no limitations."*

Photograph: All Sport

SPORTS QUIZ

1 Can you name the only country ever to have won soccer's World Cup on three occasions?

2 What are the nationalities of the three following racing drivers: a) Jody Scheckter b) Allan Jones c) Rene Arnoux?

3 Pictured below is the negative photograph of a top athlete. Can you name him?

4 What make of bike did speed king Barry Sheene (below) ride while winning the 750 cc. World Championships in 1976 and 1977?

5 At which League club did soccer superstar Kevin Keegan start his career?

6 English Tennis star John Lloyd has a very famous wife from the same sport. Can you name her?

7 The origin of the Olympic Games can be traced to which country?

8 With which sport do you associate the lovely Sharron Davies (pictured above)?

9 Pictured above is a former top sportsman as a child. Who is he (he was regarded as a bit of a knockout)?

10 How many times did Muhammad Ali win the World Heavyweight title?

11 Can you name the English cricketer who holds the record for the fastest 1,000 runs and 100 wickets in Test matches?

12 Do you know the four recognised styles in swimming competition?

★★★★★★★★★

ANSWERS

1 Brazil 2 a South African b Australian c French 3 Steve Ovett 4 Suzuki 5 Scunthorpe United 6 Chris Evert 7 Greece 8 Swimming 9 Henry Cooper 10 Three times 11 Ian Botham 12 Backstroke, breaststroke, butterfly and front crawl

CROSSWORD FUN

ACROSS

1. Stays in a tent
4. Insect flies to make a group with Gees
7. Fast engines for 'planes
9. Thrilling type of play
11. 'Parking' a boat in the sea
12. It's never quiet when there's this about
13. Send away to another land
14. In short it's television
15. What does the Queen do over her empire?
16. Where prisoners were clapped on olden day ships
17. Church tower with spire
18. What this game is
19. Board where announcements are displayed
20. Sounds like a lot of money but is actually a kind of man's voice
21. Shapes — mostly like a famous cricket ground
24. In which the ball finishes up when it's a goal
25. On which Robin Cousins is supremely good
26. Fairclough of *Coronation Street* . . .
27. . . . and Mrs. Walker from the same show
28. Second-hand
29. Like a choir is this group of musicians

DOWN

1. Kelly, Kris and Tiffany (7, 6)
2. Pictured *Magpie* man (4, 9)
3. There are usually two of these main features on *World of Sport* (6, 8)
4. It attracts fish for anglers
5. Our silver coins have a milled one
6. The Bob Monkhouse quiz (6, 8)
7. She plays Jill Harvey in *Crossroads* (4, 10)
8. Eamonn's programme (4, 2, 4, 4)
10. Pictured actor — alias Stan Ogden (8, 6)
22. Not what *The Comedians* set out to make you feel!
23. Stubbs, she was a regular in *Give Us A Clue.*

CHARLIE'S ANGELS

There are three angels whom everybody would love to have at the top of their Christmas tree, namely Charlie's!

Jaclyn Smith has been the longest serving of the original Angels trio, which comprised of herself, Farrah Fawcett-Majors and Kate Jackson. Born in Houston, Texas, Jaclyn began studying ballet at the age of 3 and took up acting at the Houston Community Playhouse while still a student at Pershing Junior High School. After moving to New York she became involved with TV commercials, while a further move to Hollywood soon saw her landing a succession of guest starring roles in popular TV series. Then came her leading part in **Charlie's Angels** which has made her a household name.

When Farrah Fawcett-Majors decided to spread her wings and concentrate on a film career, it was left to the very able Cheryl Ladd to step in and make up the numbers, a nerve-racking task. *"Suddenly I was a Charlie's Angel, one of the biggest things in television. It was great, but I had butterflies the size of elephants,"* she says.

Shelley Hack became one of the Angels when she took over from Kate Jackson. Shelley soon settled in and fully justified the confidence shown in her by the show's producers, Aaron Spelling and Leonard Goldberg, when announcing her introduction into the programme. *"We feel that Shelley has exactly the talent, style and intelligence that we are looking for."*

With three glamour angels like these gracing our television sets, you could say that we are all assured of a little Heaven on Earth!

They say that good things come in pairs, and there have certainly been plenty of famous screen couples in the world of show business over the years . . .

SEEING DOUBLE

Astaire, Laurel, Morecambe, Batman, Mork, Sapphire, Starsky. All familiar names, but they don't sound quite right, do they? Something missing perhaps? Of course! It's their other halves—Rogers, Hardy, Wise, Robin, Mindy, Steel and Hutch. Let's take a look at famous showbusiness partnerships like these and try to discover what it is that makes them inseparable . . .

'Can't act, can't sing, can dance a little.' Believe it or

Stan Laurel and Oliver Hardy.

not, that was the comment on Fred Astaire's screen test—and how he proved it wrong!

Fred's motion picture debut was made as a dancing partner for Joan Crawford in an MGM spectacular **Dancing Lady**. He was an unknown at the time but went on to meteoric fame when he teamed up with one Ginger Rogers. Together they became the biggest money-making team in screen history as they tripped the light fantastic through nine films, including probably the most famous, **Top Hat**—in which they danced the romantic **Cheek To Cheek** routine and set millions of hearts a flutter—**Follow The Fleet, Swing time, Shall We Dance** and **Carefree.** Although Fred also danced with other famous Hollywood stars—such as Rita Hayworth, Judy Garland, Audrey Hepburn and Leslie Carron, to name but a few—none has quite managed to conjure up the same magic as Ginger.

Perhaps it was the sheer simplicity of their routines, many of them were filmed in one take and all their sentimental duets were shot with the minimum of camera movement: the couple themselves provided the visual dynamics. **Cheek To Cheek** would undoubtedly have been done in a single take but Ginger's beautiful swansdown dress moulted with every twirl, ruining the continuity and messing up the Art Deco floor!

Fred and Ginger's popularity must surely owe something to the fact that they provided many a new dance for young couples of the time—and not only that it was close and romantic dancing. Ah, they don't make 'em like that any more . . !

From light-footedness to light-heartedness, and one of the most successful and best-loved American comedy teams—Laurel and Hardy.

Stan Laurel, the skinny, downtrodden, tearful one was, in fact, English. Born Stanley Jefferson in Ulverston, Lancashire, in 1890, he made his debut soon after he left school. His father, a theatre manager, who knew nothing of Stan's stage activities, decided to visit a music hall owned by a friend and, much to his amazement, discovered Stan performing there. He was dressed in his father's best trousers, cut down and patched, his frock coat and silk topper. The act went well—until Stan spotted his father and panicked. His hat fell off and he kicked it into the orchestra pit where it was squashed by the boot of a musician. As he dashed for the wings he became entangled on a steel hook and ripped half the skirt off the frock coat—and his father thought it was hilarious! He vowed from that moment on to help his son to a showbusiness career.

In 1910 Stan went to America and later started to make films, but it wasn't until 1926 that he teamed up with a large man known as Babe—Oliver Hardy. They were a huge success and, although Stan was the brains of the partnership and earned twice as much as Ollie, they were very fond of each other, obviously a great asset for two people working together, and remained great friends throughout their lifetimes. In fact, after Ollie's death in 1957, Stan said that 'he was like a brother to me'. And contrary to their famous catch-phrase, in real life, Ollie never had cause to say 'That's another fine mess you've gotten me into, Stanley!'

When Laurel and Hardy made their last tour of Britain in 1953, two aspiring young comedians were among those who queued for tickets at the Embassy Theatre, Peterborough. Their names? Eric Morecambe and Ernie Wise. They were virtually reared on a diet of Laurel and Hardy films and reckon they've seen practically every movie they made.

Both Eric, the one with the glasses, and Ernie, the one with the short, fat, hairy legs, were child discoveries and first met in a variety show at Swansea when they were fourteen-years-old. Soon they were inseparable friends and have been so ever since. *"In forty years there has never been any written contract between us,"* says Ernie. *"We trust each other and we share a relationship which is totally fulfilling."*

At the beginning of their career together, for a while their roles were reversed. Ernie was the comic and Eric the Wellma Boy. The 'Wellma Boy'? He's the one who 'feeds' the comic—he comes on stage and says *'Wellma boy, and what are you going to do tonight?"*!

They were forced to split up during the war years but when Ernie came back from the Merchant Navy and Eric from his time as a Bevan Boy (down the mines where his heart trouble began) they switched roles and Mr. Wise became the Wellma Boy. They've never looked back.

When talking of comedy teams, you can't, of course, not mention other such successful duos as The Two Ronnies—Ronnie Barker and Ronnie Corbett—and Little and Large, but in terms of the amount of time they've been treading the boards together, they're mere youngsters compared to Eric and Ernie.

And talking of youngsters in the comedy >>>> →

Reared on a diet of Laurel and Hardy films: Eric and Ern.

Astaire and Rogers in typical pose.

Eric and Ernie.

Robin Williams and Pam Dawber
Mork and Mindy

**Joanna Lumley and
David McCallum**
Sapphire & Steel

⟫⟫⟫ → business, there's one recently-formed American partnership that can boast of being out of this world—or at least half of it—and that's **Mork and Mindy.** Mork, played by Robin Williams, is from the planet Ork and unaccustomed to our Earthly ways—he sits on his head, drinks through his forefinger and holds philosophical discussions with eggs! His flat-mate and protector is Mindy, played by Pam Dawber, who tries to keep him out of trouble.

Robin, born in Edinburgh, Scotland, is just as zany when he's not playing Mork and is highly respected for his own special brand of humour and overwhelming personality. Equipped with what has been described as a 'kaleidoscopic' face, Robin constantly improvises on the **Mork and Mindy** scripts. Pam says: *"Most of the time, I don't know what Robin's going to do. I end up laughing hysterically, and sometimes it's a miracle we get the scenes shot before I blow it all!"*

With Mindy being the sensible half of the duo, it might seem to follow that Pam would be a more serious person than Robin. But the truth is that they both break up regularly on the set, clowning around as much as possible! *"And,"* says Pam, *"we get along beautifully."*

Another 'out of this world' couple are **Sapphire And Steel**, and they're far from being a comedy act!

They call themselves 'agents', and their purpose is to battle against time and the dark forces of the unknown. No-one knows where they come from or exactly who they are, but they appear whenever they're needed—and they disappear just as mysteriously when they've won the fight. Sapphire is able to actually stop time—and turn it backwards and forwards—and when she concentrates hard her eyes turn an incredible bright blue (sapphire, in fact; hence the name). And Steel? As

his name suggests, he has the power to change hi enemies into a substance as hard as steel and rende them harmless.

Sapphire, of course, is the lovely Joanna Lumley and Steel is played by David McCallum (who sever: years ago was one half of another successful duo in **Th Man From U.N.C.L.E.** with Robert Vaughn). It's th first time that they've worked together but it soo became obvious that something had 'clicked' betwee them. As Joanna said when the show was first made: " think we'll do well together. We've certainly enjoye working with each other."

Rather more down-to-earth, but equally as successfu at crime-fighting are Batman and Robin—the cape crusaders.

To all but their butler, Alfred, Bruce Wayne, multi millionaire head of the Wayne Foundation, and hi

Batman and Robin.

Cat and mouse team – *Tom And Jerry*.

His idea has always been to concentrate much more on the relationship between the two friends—after all, that's what makes **Starsky And Hutch** much more than just another cop series.

And Paul thinks it's very important that they can identify with the characters they play and as they are very close off screen, too, it comes easily to them. It was Paul, in fact, who gave David an immense amount of support when he had a skiing accident whilst shooting a sequence for a film he was making. David was on his back in hospital in Colorado for months getting more and more depressed over the fear that he might not walk again.

"When Paul heard how depressed I was getting," says David, *"he kept making flying visits to my hospital bed, and what a visitor! Paul will always have a job waiting for him as a comedian if his acting doesn't last! He used to make me laugh so much, that even lying there on my back I got to see the funny side of things."*

And so David, with more than a little help from Paul, got back on his feet again to continue the partnership.

A couple famous for being on the other side of the law are Butch Cassidy and The Sundance Kid, notorious train-robbers. Not a particularly lovable pair in their own life-times, they were immortalised on celluloid by two of the great Hollywood stars—Paul Newman and Robert Redford. Their partnership was so successful that they went on to play another couple of crooks (naughty but nice ones!) in **The Sting**. Who said that crime doesn't pay!

And finally, how could we leave out the most famous cartoon double act—**Tom And Jerry**? What makes them so different is that, unlike all the other duos we've mentioned who work together, these two are in constant battle against each other, with Tom, the cat, forever dreaming of making a tasty meal of Jerry, the mouse! However, Jerry is always a good deal ahead of Tom in every way and always lives to see another day!

That's teamwork!

young ward, Dick Grayson, are just ordinary, law-abiding folk. But when they get a call for help on the Batphone, they immediately head for the secret entrance to the Batpoles (it's behind a bookcase in the den) and slide down to the Batcave. A few seconds later, after a slick, quick change into their Batgear, they're pursuing the crooks in their Batmobile.

In real life, Batman is Adam West and Robin is Burt Ward, and through the show they've become superstars.

From the Splats! Pows! and Kapows! of the dynamic duo to the more realistic crime-fighting in the streets of Los Angeles by Supercops **Starsky And Hutch.** At one time the series was condemned for being too violent but because the stars, Paul Michael Glaser and David Soul felt strongly about it, the violence was cut down to a minimum. David, in fact, has done several lectures in the States about the worrying crime rate.

Butch Cassidy and The Sundance Kid:
Paul Newman (left) and Robert Redford.

TOM BAKER

"I didn't really come from a book-reading class," says Tom Baker, *"but now it's become one of my main interests."*

And that's why Tom is not only the tremendously popular, time-travelling **Dr. Who,** but also the host of one of ITV's most absorbing children's shows, **The Book Tower.**

Born in Liverpool in 1933, Tom spent six years of his life—between the ages of 15 and 21—as a monk in a strict order in Jersey. A large part of his acting career was taken up with The National Theatre, and he first caught the attention of the Television public when he appeared as Rasputin. Then, of course, he went on to play the part that has made him instantly recognisable—**Dr. Who.**

How did the viewers of **The Book Tower** take to Tom in his newest role, after getting so used to him as the Doctor? *"The reaction was utterly positive,"* he says. *"For example, for the early 1980 series, we put out rather nice posters to promote it, and these went into libraries and schools. Before any of the shows actually went out, we had something like 8,000 requests for the posters, which indicated a marvellous advance interest in the series."*

All of which goes to show the amazing popularity of Tom Baker.

Back to his playing of the Doctor: *"I'm very interested in what frightens children. I deliberately try and find the points where they will be frightened—I think sometimes I can locate the points in the script where young viewers will be ducking behind the sofa, or under the table, or hiding behind cushions. I also add humour to the situation, of course, so the children are confident that behind the trouble I might be in, I'll get through in the end.*

"Heroes always do."

LAUGH-IN

Q) What did the painting say to the wall?
A) First they framed me, then they hung me.

Pam: **My teacher does bird imitations.**
Sam: Really?
Pam: **Yes. She watches me like a hawk.**

Jack: **I've changed my mind.**
Jill: I'm so pleased to hear it. Does the new one work any better?

Q) What do hedgehogs eat with cheese?
A) Prickled onions.

FRED SMITH FRENCH POLISHER

"Parlez vous english?"

MORRIS

INLAND REVENUE

"I don't think he jumped, I think he was pushed."

Q) Who sings at big hotels?
A) Hilton John.

Diner: **Waiter, what's wrong with these eggs?**
Waiter: Don't ask me—I only laid the table.

1st Eskimo: **Can I kiss your wife?**
2nd Eskimo: Sure, it's no skin off my nose.

Q) What do you give a sick bird?
A) Tweetment.

This background picture shows a section of the longest wall ever built—The Great Wall of China. It was built in the Ming Dynasty (12th and 13th centuries) by one-third of the nation's able-bodied men. The thousands who died from the strenuous work were buried underneath it, hence its nickname: the longest cemetery on earth.

These junks (above) are pictured sailing the Li River in the south of China.

These children (right), aged between 3 and 6, board at a kindergarten for six days a week, leaving their mothers free to work for the country.

A bit different to your own classroom, no doubt, but this is a typical place of learning for the Chinese youngsters.

Pictured above right is the form of transport widely used in the rural areas. This young lady (right) is putting on a special display as a welcome to some Western visitors.

Colour photographs by Peter Bolton

You must have seen and heard a lot about China this year, with that country's growing involvement in sports and other events. Perhaps you've wondered what all the fuss is about? After all, you might think, it's just another nation taking part in world affairs. But is it? To most older people in Britain and the western world, China has been a completely unknown place for many years, with hardly any films or photographs available to show what life is like there, and strict secrecy surrounding the most ordinary day to day activities. So that's what the excitement is about—we're seeing the 'opening-up' of a country that for so long has been a mystery to us. Over the page we look at this fascinating land . . .

SPOTLIGHT ON CHINA

No individual person in China owns a private car so everyone travels by bicycle. It's cheap (they each cost around £30) and avoids traffic jams.

This lady is working in a rattan factory where they make cane baskets and chairs, etc. She takes home around £20 a month.

These farm workers (left), who start at about 6.30 am and finish when it gets dark, get just one day off a week—it sounds like hard work, but no-one goes hungry.

This company of dancers (above) give a demonstration of their art.

WHAT is 1,500 miles long, took 2,000 years to build, and is the only man-made structure on earth which is visible from the moon? Answer: The Great Wall of China, a formidable barrier which lies across the north face of South-East Asia like a giant petrified snake.

And, until recently, you would have had to be an astronaut to see the mighty wall. Like everything else in China, it was barred to Western eyes. Not for some 40 years had any but a privileged few been allowed to cross the forbidden frontier.

The only native Chinese we saw were inscrutable table tennis players, who turned up at international tournaments, hit unstoppable serves, and slipped silently back behind the Bamboo Curtain with the trophies. All we heard about this country of 960 million people came from dated news reports which told vaguely of earthquakes and typhoons, floods and droughts and political upheavals.

Changes

Now all that is changing and businessmen and tourists are being welcomed to China in increasing numbers. They are seeing a strangely different world—just as Marco Polo did in the 13th century, when he travelled 7,500 miles overland to China from his native Venice and returned with incredible stories of his adventures.

He told how Chinese astronomers had built observatories, discovered new stars, and recorded eclipses of the sun since 4,000 B.C.; about the country's paper currency—at that time, heavy metal coins were the norm elsewhere—

and high standard of living, and how they had invented gunpowder.

Today's visitors are more surprised by the Chinese way of life than by scientific achievements. The Western traveller is escorted through China by official guides and his journey, and what he will see, is decided beforehand by the Chinese government. He will probably glimpse the Great Wall, the tombs of the Ming Emperors, the spectacular scenery and gorges of Kweilin, mountains, and great rivers like the Yangtze.

But although he won't be able to choose his route, the visitor to China will see Peking—everyone is taken there.

Surprises

And it's in this ancient city that the surprises really begin. The hotels are mammoth by Western standards, with often more than a thousand visitors teeming like soldier ants. Although you get a key to your room, there's no need to lock the door, because the Chinese are among the most honest people in the world and theft is virtually unknown.

Arrive at your hotel in spring—the temperature can be near freezing—and you'll have to go to dinner in your overcoat, but visitors are usually warmed when they receive their hotel bills—the rates are the lowest in the world.

Step out of the hotel and the noise of Peking will deafen you. Great armies of cyclists, all ringing their bells, wobble down the centre of the road—no one keeps to the left or right in the Peking free-for-all—weaving around the state-owned cars and khaki buses, whose drivers respond with ear-splitting blasts on

the horn.

The pedestrians put on their own show for Western visitors. Walk a few hundred yards and you'll attract a crowd because tourists are still a novelty. And don't be surprised when everyone claps their hands it's the traditional Chinese greeting.

Peking isn't all noise and bustle Visit the brilliantly coloured ancient buildings, such as the Temple of Heaven with its yellow, green and blue-tiled roof, the Summer Palace and the Forbidden City, and you'll feel a sense of space. In fact, there are many parks, where the Chinese gather to do their exercises.

Regular exercise, like so many things in China, is compulsory Clothes, for example—before they reach their teens, children can wear colourful outfits. But later, at an age when British teenagers are shopping for the newest styles, the Chinese are wriggling into the regulation blue or grey cotton jacket and trousers—and both sexes wear the same.

Nor is there time in the young Chinese girl's diary to worry about make-up. It's not fashionable and with the government telling her what to study, and a six-day work

...g week, she has to rely on soap and water for her complexion.

Courtship

She believes that to be attractive to a boy she must work hard and study hard. If she has spare time for a date, she and her boyfriend will go for walks or attend cultural concerts. If they watch television, they will only see news programmes, and whereas Western couples will play records or go to a disco, their Chinese counterparts will be taking in a discussion group.

Young Chinese aren't allowed to marry when they wish. Boys in the towns must wait until they are 27, the girls until they are 25. If they live in a country region, however, they can marry two years earlier. Once they settle down to married life, the smaller their family the better the government likes it, with only-children getting a free state education.

The government also decides who will go to university and what work they will do when they leave. Everyone works a six-day week, taking time off by rota, so the Chinese calendar must be the only one in the world with seven Sun-days each week. And, of course, every day starts with that compulsory exercise . . .

If the exercise fails to keep you fit, you are likely to receive acupuncture. This is an ancient form of healing where needles are applied to parts of the body to relieve rheumatism, reduce weight, and to cure tiredness. Acupuncture is also used as a local anaesthetic and brain surgery has been carried out while the patient eats an apple, or chats to the doctors.

While China might seem in some ways to live in the past—hotels put lace doilies on the tables and Victorian-style antimacassars (ornamental coverings) on the chairs—there are signs that Western ideas are beginning to catch on. At the end of last year, assistants from a Shanghai department store modelled French fashions in Peking. Most members of the audience still wore modified versions of the blue uniform of this era, but the show received hearty applause. Other Western imports include cola and skateboards, and one couple were seen dancing the tango in a Shanghai conference centre recently.

Don't be tempted to take China's lifting of the Bamboo Curtain for granted: it might be a country of some four million square miles, with mountain ranges, vast plains and mighty rivers, but it has a habit of vanishing.

The Romans discovered the great Chinese Vanishing Trick in the 6th century A.D. Until then, they had imported their silk from the Orient. Then with silkworms smuggled into Italy the Romans began their own silk industry. No longer needing to travel east, they forgot China and it was not until Marco Polo, five centuries later, that the country was re-discovered.

Even then, the imperial dynasties, who ruled China until 1912, weren't noted for their hospitality to foreigners and the great country has, until now, remained a mysterious and remote land.

No wonder, then, that the Chinese are noted for their puzzles.

(Above left to right) Terraced hillsides in Tachai; a toy department in a Peking store; and fishy business at Chanchiang harbour. (Below) Chinese Junks crowd the water: a scene that hasn't changed for hundreds of years.

If you've just been reading about China (and even if you haven't!) consider this: ten years or so ago, you probably wouldn't even have heard of such Chinese foods as chow mein & chop suey, or Italian ones like spaghetti & pizzas, or Greek ones like kebabs. Nor would you have seen peculiar American ice cream & milk shake flavours or giant hamburgers with all the trimmings. But now, they're all part of the world-wide character of our food in Britain . . .

IT'S A TASTY WORLD!

If you could travel back a decade in time you probably wouldn't have found a single take-away in your local High Street except for the British fish and chip shop. But look today and curry restaurants, hamburger houses, kebab and Chinese restaurants are all there in between the food, electrical and furniture shops. And there aren't many high streets these days without an American ice cream parlour.

I can remember when it all started with coffee bars in the 1950s. These were the *in* places for teenagers, who used to sit and talk, sipping coffee called cappucino which is espresso, or black coffee, with milk. The coffee and the gleaming chromed machines that hissed as they heated the milk were imported from Italy. Soon came curry restaurants for the Indians who came to this country from Kenya, in Africa, and from the Indian continent. Though you might find curry too spicy and hot for you, I bet you enjoy pizzas, an Italian favourite, and kebabs, a Greek speciality.

But my favourite of all are the hamburgers—the most convenient quick meal, with protein to sustain us through the day. We've got our Wimpy Bars, but the Americans boasted that their hamburgers were bigger and better, their milk shakes thicker and fluffier and set out to prove it. Now among the latest of all the imports from other parts of the world are the ice-cream parlours advertising 32 flavours with scrumptious sounding names like English Toffee, Blueberry Cheesecake and Nutty Chocolate.

Even though all of these foreign dishes look so different from our own English food, the ingredients are often very familiar, meat, fish and veg. just cooked a new way so you can make them yourself at home. Try our ice-cream recipe, make hamburgers for lunch, then when you've got some time, perhaps at the weekends, surprise your mum with your own version of a pizza.

In *Turkey*, as well as i *Greece*, the name kebab i used for grilled meat an vegetables cooked on skewer over charcoal. Cube of vegetables or pieces o fish can be used instead o meat. Here, we've taken lamb kebab and added mush rooms, onions and gree peppers served with rice t make an interesting meal.

LAMB KEBABS
(serves 4)

225g (8oz.) very small onions
salt
225g (8oz.) Patna rice
1 small green pepper
2 large tomatoes
125g (4oz.) button mushrooms
4 thick lamb chump chops
8 bay leaves
cooking oil

Skin the onions. Put into a sauce pan containing about 2.5cm (1 inch of boiling salted water. Reduce th heat and simmer for 10 minutes until tender. Drain. Boil 1.1 litre (2 pints) of salted water in a larg saucepan. Add the rice and coo gently for 12 minutes. Meanwhile wash the pepper, halve and remov the seeds. Cut the flesh into 2.5c (1 inch) pieces. Wash the tomato and cut into quarters. Wash th mushrooms. You don't have to pe them when they are very smal Wipe the chops. Remove mea from the bones and cut into bit sized pieces. Thread vegetable meat and bay leaves alternately long skewers. Brush with oil. La skewers in the grill pan. Coo under a hot grill for 10–12 minute turning skewers occasionally t

...ook the meat on all sides. Drain
...he rice in a sieve then run hot
...ater through it to separate the
...rains. Spoon rice into a serving
...late, lay kebabs on top. Serve hot.

...he *Danish* are famed
...or their open sandwiches,
...hich may be served as
...nacks, as a starter to a
...eal, or several of them
...ay make a complete
...eal. There are hundreds
...f varieties and new ones
...re turning up all the time.
...he sandwiches, called
...morrebrod, range from
...imple ones to very elabo-
...ate compositions which are
...vailable in delicatessens
...nd restaurants.

SCANDINAVIAN SLICE

(serves 2)
210g (7oz.) can mackerel fillets
2 large lettuce leaves
...ml (1 level teaspoon) horseradish
sauce
...0ml (2 tablespoons) natural yogurt
4 gherkins
25g (1oz.) butter
2 slices brown bread
8 cucumber slices

...pen the can of mackerel fillets and
...rain them well. Wash and dry the
...ettuce leaves. Stir the horseradish
...nto the yogurt and mix well to-
...ether. Slice the gherkins. Butter
...he bread and cover each slice with
... lettuce leaf. Place a cucumber
...ice at each corner of the bread
...ice. Arrange mackerel fillets on
...op. Spoon the yogurt mixture
...etween the mackerel fillets. Garn-
...h with slices of gherkin.

Here's an easy-to-make *American-style* ice-cream.

FUDGE AND RAISIN ICE CREAM

(serves 4)
2 chocolate covered fudge fingers
397g (14oz.) can condensed milk
150ml (¼ pint) milk
50g (2oz.) raisins

Set refrigerator or freezing compartment to coldest setting. Cut the
fudge fingers in small pieces. Stir
the milk into the condensed milk
and whisk for 2 minutes. Add the
fudge and raisins. Mix well. Pour
into an ice tray. Cover with foil and
place in freezing compartment. Stir
after 1 hour and leave to freeze.

Croques Monsieur originated
in *France*. Try this version
using pasta, cream cheese
and chutney for an interesting snack or supper dish.

PASTA CROQUES MONSIEUR

(serves 4)
8 large slices of bread
125g (4oz.) cream cheese
30ml (2 tablespoons) chutney
2 eggs, size 3
150ml (¼ pint) milk
salt and pepper
50g (2oz.) butter
439g (15½oz.) can spaghetti in
tomato sauce

Spread bread with cream cheese
and chutney. Sandwich slices together in pairs. Cut in half diagonal-
ly. Beat eggs with milk and season-
ing, and dip each sandwich into the
mixture. Fry on both sides in
melted butter until crisp and
golden. Meanwhile heat spaghetti
in a pan. Top each cooked "Croques Monsieur" with hot spaghetti
and serve immediately.

Pizza is the *Italian* word for
'pie'. It is derived from a
round of yeast dough spread
with tomatoes and mozza-
rella cheese and baked in a
hot oven. Here we've added
some bacon to make it tasty
and we've used a scone base
for our quick pizza.

QUICK PIZZA

(serves 4)
1 small onion
65g (2½ oz.) butter or margarine
213g (7½ oz.) can tomatoes
15ml (1 tablespoon) tomato puree
salt and pepper
50g (2oz.) Cheddar cheese
6 rashers streaky bacon
3 stuffed olives
225g (8oz.) self-raising flour
150ml (¼ pint) milk

Skin and chop onions. Melt 15g
(½oz.) butter in a saucepan, add the
onions and fry for 5 minutes. Stir in
canned tomatoes and tomato puree
and simmer uncovered for about 10
minutes to reduce liquid by half.
Season with salt and pepper. Cool
slightly. Grate the cheese. Remove
the rinds from the bacon. Cut the
olives in half. Grease a baking
sheet. Sift flour and 5ml (1 level
teaspoon) salt together in a bowl.
Rub in the remaining butter until
mixture looks like fine bread-
crumbs. Add the milk and mix to
form a soft dough. Roll into a 2.5cm
(9 inch) round and place on the
baking sheet. Spread tomato mixture on top of scone base to within
2.5cm (1 inch) of the edge. Arrange
the bacon radiating out from the
centre and sprinkle cheese on top.
Garnish with stuffed olive halves.
Bake at 200°C (400°F) or gas mark 6
for 20 minutes until dough is risen
and golden.

GUESS WHO?

At first glance, the faces shown here may mean nothing to you. But take a closer look—hidden behind each disguise is a star of stage, screen or radio. See if you can unmask each celebrity; if you're beaten by any of the famous faces in "fancy dress", then check the answers which you can find at the bottom of the page.

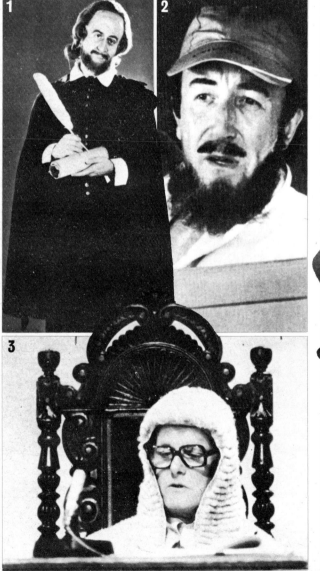

TISWAS TWOSOME

Any regular viewer of ATV's madcap *Tiswas* on Saturday mornings will know all about the crazy banter that takes place on that anything-goes show.

Well here's a chance for you to invent your own "Tiswas-talk". Just fill in the captions we've conveniently left you on the two pictures printed here, featuring Bob Carolgees and his faithful hound Spit (with friend), and presenters Chris Tarrant and Sally James (with foot).

They all had their own hilarious comments to make at the time—but *Tiswas* the opportunity you wanted to create your own funny captions . . .

★★★★★★★★★★★★★★

A dramatic moment from a
Benny Hill Show, as Benny
inches his way up a sheer
brick wall with only a
thin rope for support . . .

. . . and the mad bomber's
there, too, clinging desperately
to that life-saving rope . . .

. . . but what's this?
She's let go!
She's leaning backwards . .